Sunday Morning Blend

VOLUME 3

Hymns plus Praise & Worship Songs
Includes Chord Symbols

Sunday Morning Blend

VOLUME 3

Hymns plus Praise & Worship Songs
Includes Chord Symbols

Arranged by
Carol Tornquist

EDITED BY
CAROL TORNQUIST & KEN BARKER

ORIGINAL COVER DESIGN BY
POLLEI DESIGN

MUSIC ENGRAVED BY
RIC SIMENSON

WORD MUSIC®

All about Sunday Morning Blend, Volume 3 . . .

The first volume of SUNDAY MORNING BLEND was published in 2000 . . . the second one in 2002 . . . and so 2004 seemed like the perfect time to create Volume 3! This 'blended worship' concept continues to work well for those of you who embrace contemporary praise & worship music, but don't want to give up our rich heritage of hymns.

As in the previous two folios, these hymns have been given a more contemporary feel . . . sometimes re-harmonized, syncopated or even written in a new meter altogether . . . to make the 'musical connection' work. Each arrangement includes chord symbols as well, in case you want to invite some other instrumentalists to play along. Or, you may use the chord symbols to get creative with what is already on the written page!

Remember that all of these melodies (regardless of the century in which they were written!) are the "psalms, hymns and spiritual songs" referred to in Colossians 3:16. So may they all *dwell in you richly* as you play them.

Carol Tornquist

Carol Tornquist

Contents

in alphabetical order

Breathe
with Fill Me Now

Words and Music by
MARIE BARNETT
Arranged by Carol Tornquist

8

FILL ME NOW *(Words: ELWOOD H. STOKES / Music: JOHN R. SWENEY)*

Let Everything That Has Breath

with All Creatures of Our God and King

WORDS AND MUSIC BY
MATT REDMAN
Arranged by Carol Tornquist

Bright four (♩ = ca. 112)

All Creatures of Our God and King *(Words: St. FRANCIS of Assisi; Music: Geistliche Kirchengsange)*

Forever
with The Love of God

WORDS AND MUSIC BY
CHRIS TOMLIN
Arranged by Carol Tornquist

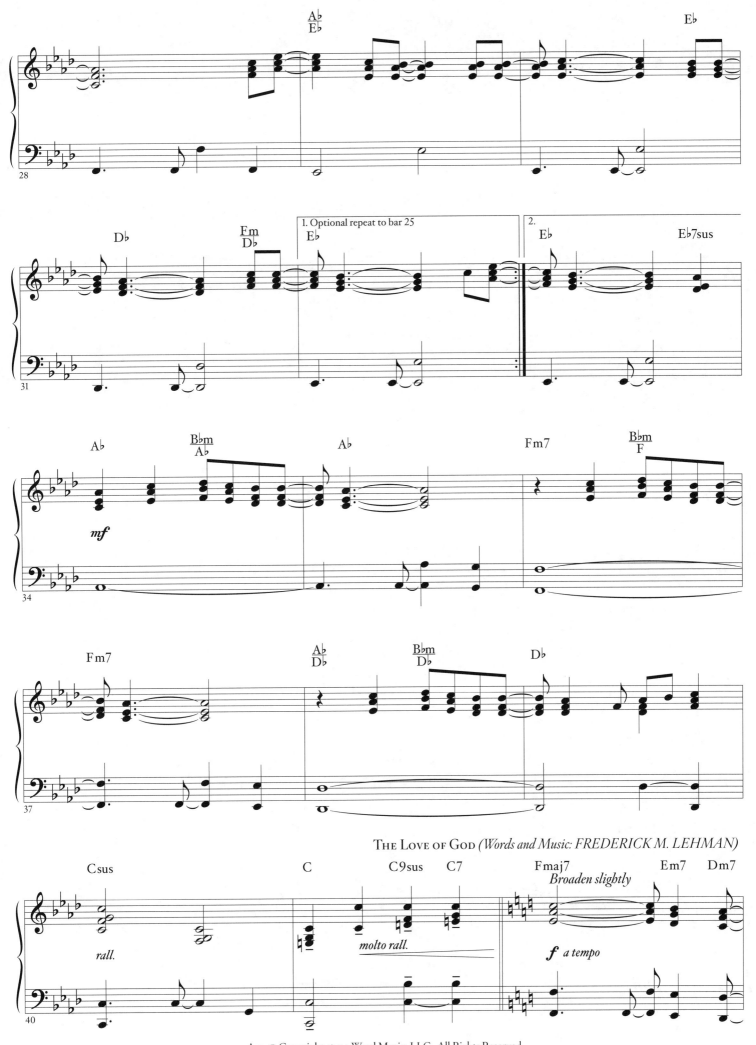

THE LOVE OF GOD *(Words and Music: FREDERICK M. LEHMAN)*

Here I Am to Worship

with Fairest Lord Jesus

WORDS AND MUSIC BY
TIM HUGHES
Arranged by Carol Tornquist

Fairest Lord Jesus *(Words: German hymn; Music: Schlesische Volkslieder)*

Shout to the North

with O for a Thousand Tongues to Sing

WORDS AND MUSIC BY
MARTIN SMITH
Arranged by Carol Tornquist

O for a Thousand Tongues to Sing *(Words: CHARLES WESLEY; Music: CARL G. GLAZER)*

(SHOUT TO THE NORTH)

Refiner's Fire

with Take Time to Be Holy

WORDS AND MUSIC BY
BRIAN DOERKSEN
Arranged by Carol Tornquist

32

Take Time to Be Holy *(Words: WILLIAM D. LONGSTAFF; Music: GEORGE C. STEBBINS)*

(Bring out L.H.)

Better Is One Day
with Come into His Presence

WORDS AND MUSIC BY
MATT REDMAN
Arranged by Carol Tornquist

Lightly syncopated (♩ = ca. 69)

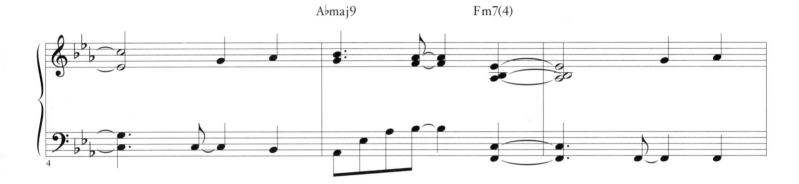

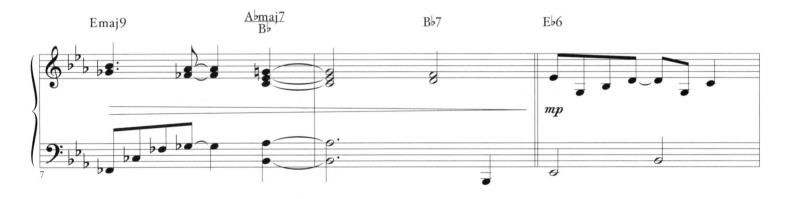

38

COME INTO HIS PRESENCE *(Unknown)*

You Are My King (Amazing Love)

with Love Divine, All Loves Excelling

Words and Music by
BILLY JAMES FOOTE
Arranged by Carol Tornquist

42

Love Divine, All Loves Excelling *(Words: CHARLES WESLEY / Music: JOHN ZUNDEL)*

Cry of My Heart
with I'll Go Where You Want Me to Go

Words and Music by
TERRY BUTLER
Arranged by Carol Tornquist

Lightly syncopated (♩ = ca. 94)

I'll Go Where You Want Me to Go *(Words: MARY BROWN / Music: CARRIE E. ROUNSEFELL)*

The Wonderful Cross
with The Old Rugged Cross

Hymn by ISAAC WATTS
Words and Music by
CHRIS TOMLIN, JESSE REEVES & J. D. WALT

Arranged by Carol Tornquist

Legato, with reverence (♩ = ca. 86)

(When I Survey the Wondrous Cross)

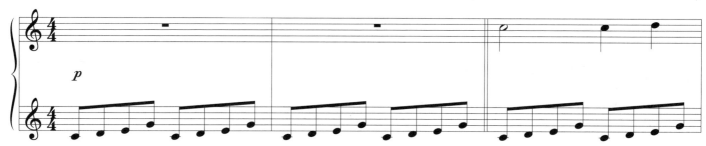

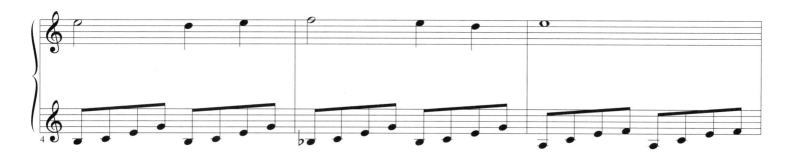

(THE WONDERFUL CROSS)

(When I Survey the Wondrous Cross)

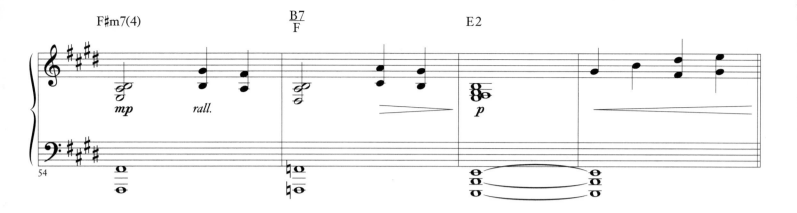

The Old Rugged Cross *(Words & Music: GEORGE BENNARD)*

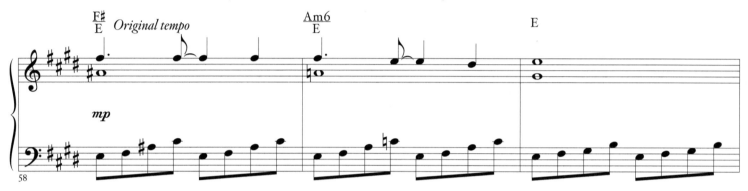

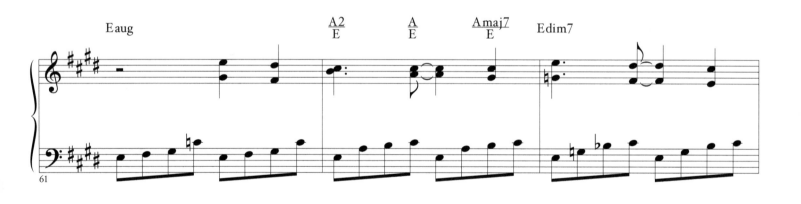

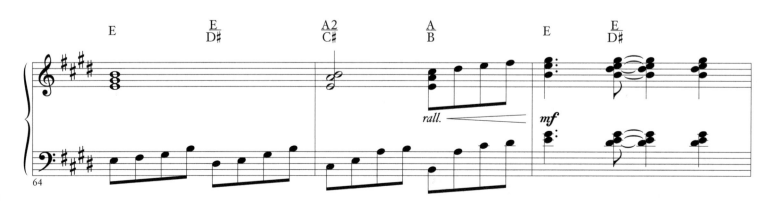

Did You Feel the Mountains Tremble?

with Alleluia! Alleluia!

WORDS AND MUSIC BY
MARKIN SMITH
Arranged by Carol Tornquist

With energy! (♩ = ca. 106)

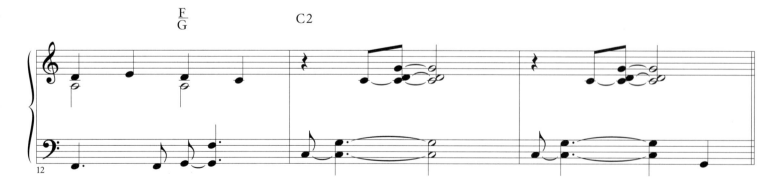

ALLELUIA! ALLELUIA! *(Words: CHRISTOPHER WORDSWORTH; Music: LUDWIG VAN BEETHOVEN)*

Let My Words Be Few

with My Jesus, I Love Thee

WORDS AND MUSIC BY
MATT and BETH REDMAN
Arranged by Carol Tornquist

With simplicity (♩ = ca. 80)

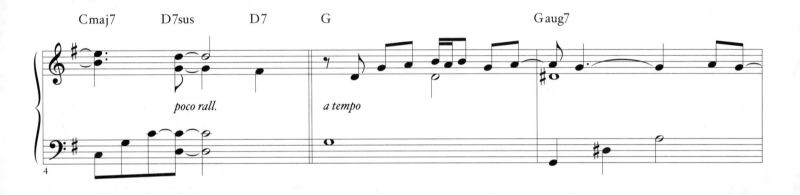

My Jesus, I Love Thee *(Words: WILLIAM. R. FEATHERSTON; Music: ADONIRAM J. GORDON)*

Holy and Anointed One
with Christ, We Do All Adore Thee

Words and Music by
JOHN BARNETT
Arranged by Carol Tornquist

Reverently (♩ = ca. 84)

70

CHRIST, WE DO ALL ADORE THEE *(Words: Adoramus Te; Music: THEODORE DUBOIS)*

Simply (slightly slower tempo)

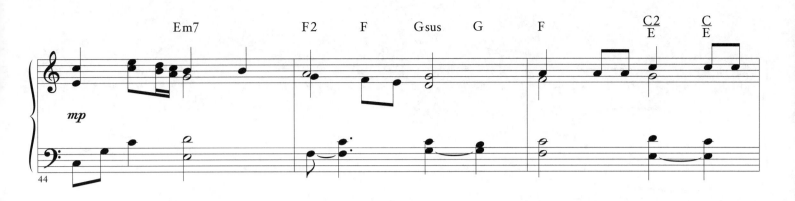

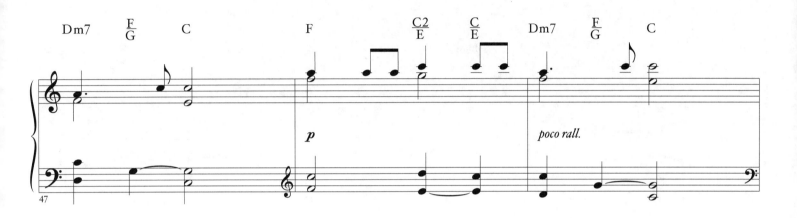

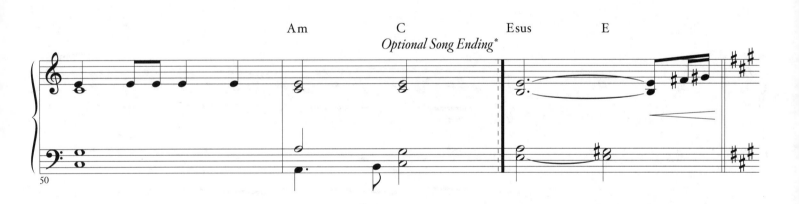

(Holy and Anointed One)

* Add *rit.* in bar 51 when using the optional song ending.

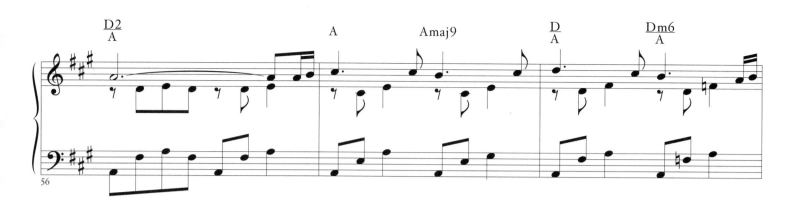

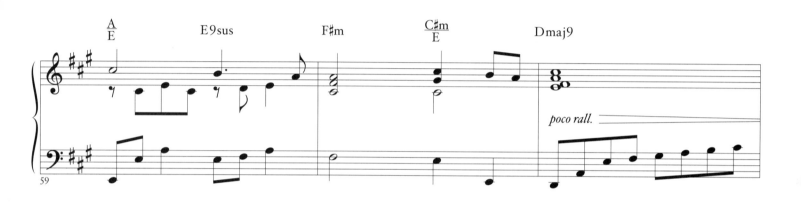

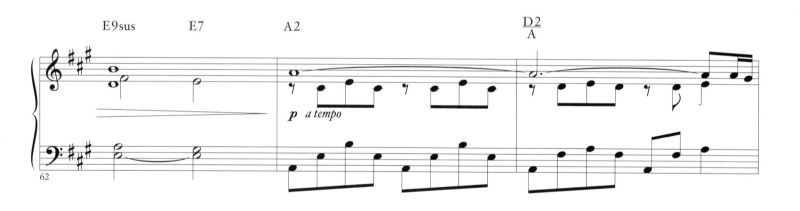

We Want to See Jesus Lifted High

with Jesus Shall Reign

WORDS AND MUSIC BY
DOUG HORLEY
Arranged by Carol Tornquist

Jesus Shall Reign *(Words: ISAAC WATTS; Music: JOHN HATTON)*

Once Again
with What a Wonderful Savior!

Words and Music by
MATT REDMAN
Arranged by Carol Tornquist

What a Wonderful Savior! *(Words & Music: ELISHA A. HOFFMAN)*

Word of God, Speak

with Break Thou the Bread of Life

WORDS AND MUSIC BY
PETER KIPLEY & BART MILLARD
Arranged by Carol Tornquist

Break Thou the Bread of Life *(Words: MARY A. LATHBURY; Music: WILLIAM F. SHERWIN)*

(WORD OF GOD, SPEAK)

Holy, Holy, Holy

with Holy, Holy, Holy! Lord God Almighty

WORDS AND MUSIC BY
GARY OLIVER
Arranged by Carol Tornquist

Holy! Holy! Holy! Lord God Almighty *(Words: REGINALD HEBER; Music: JOHN B. DYKES)*

Oh, the Glory of Your Presence

with Jesus, the Very Thought of Thee

WORDS AND MUSIC BY
STEVE FRY
Arranged by Carol Tornquist

Slowly and thoughtfully (♩ = ca. 72)

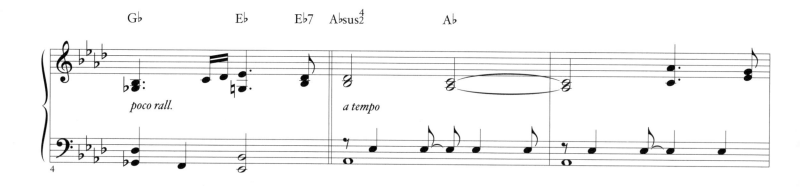

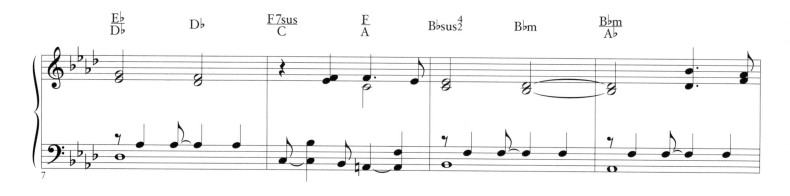

Jesus, the Very Thought of Thee *(Words: Attr. to BERNARD of Clairvaux; Music: JOHN B. DYKES)*

Change My Heart, Oh God

with Cleanse Me

WORDS AND MUSIC BY
EDDIE ESPINOSA
Arranged by Carol Tornquist

Cleanse Me *(Words: J. EDWIN ORR / Music: Maori melody)*

In the Presence of Jehovah
with Like a River Glorious

WORDS AND MUSIC BY
GERON and BECKY DAVIS
Arranged by Carol Tornquist

Like a River Glorious *(Words: FRANCES HAVERGAL; Music: JAMES MOUNTAIN)*

(In the Presence of Jehovah)

You Are So Good to Me

with God Is So Good

WORDS AND MUSIC BY
DON CHAFFER, BEN & ROBIN PASLEY
Arranged by Carol Tornquist

Moderate four (♩ = ca. 80)

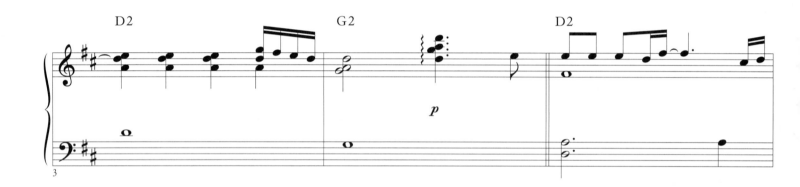

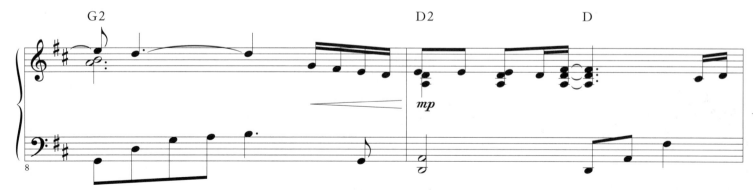

God Is So Good *(Traditional)*

We Fall Down

with Praise God from Whom All Blessings Flow

WORDS AND MUSIC BY
CHRIS TOMLIN
Arranged by Carol Tornquist

Praise God from Whom All Blessings Flow *(Words: THOMAS KEN; Music: Geistliche Kirchengesange)*

Take My Life

with Take My Life and Let It Be Consecrated

WORDS AND MUSIC BY
SCOTT UNDERWOOD
Arranged by Carol Tornquist

Easy and lightly syncopated ($\quarternote$ = ca. 72)

Take My Life and Let It Be Consecrated *(Words: FRANCES R. HAVERGAL; Music: HENRY A. CESAR MALAN)*

(Take My Life)

The Power of Your Love

with My Savior's Love

WORDS AND MUSIC BY
GEOFF BULLOCK
Arranged by Carol Tornquist

My Savior's Love *(Words & Music: CHARLES H. GABRIEL)*

Who Can Satisfy My Soul Like You?

with Blessed Assurance

WORDS AND MUSIC BY
DENNIS L. JERNIGAN
Arranged by Carol Tornquist

Blessed Assurance *(Words: FANNY J. CROSBY; Music: PHOEBE K. KNAPP)*

Notes

Chord Symbols

The following chord symbols are included for those accompanists whose musical background emphasized "reading what was on the page" more than understanding music theory and harmony. The key of C Major is used as a "model" on the following 2 pages, *but the same "rules" apply in any major key.*

TYPES OF CHORDS*	CHORD SYMBOL
MAJOR (letter name only)	C
MINOR (letter name plus 'm')	Cm
AUGMENTED (letter name plus 'aug')	Caug (or C+)
AUGMENTED SEVEN (letter name plus 'aug7')	Caug7 (or C+7)
DIMINISHED (letter name plus 'dim')	Cdim (or C°)
DIMINISHED SEVEN (letter name plus 'dim7')	Cdim7 (or C°7)
SUSPENDED (letter name plus 'sus')	Csus
SUSPENDED 4,2 (letter name plus 'sus $\frac{4}{2}$')	Csus$\frac{4}{2}$
MAJOR WITH ADDED 2 (letter name plus '2')	C2
MAJOR WITH ADDED 6 (letter name plus '6')	C6
DOMINANT SEVEN (letter name plus '7')	C7
NINE (letter name plus '9')	C9
DOMINANT SEVEN SUSPENDED (letter name plus '7 sus')	C7sus
DOMINANT SEVEN FLAT NINE (letter name plus '7♭9')	C7♭9
MINOR SIX (letter name plus 'm6')	Cm6
MINOR SEVEN (letter name plus 'm7')	Cm7
MINOR SEVEN FLAT FIVE (letter name plus 'm7♭5')	Cm7♭5
MINOR SEVEN WITH ADDED FOUR (letter name plus 'm7(4)')	Cm7(4)
MAJOR SEVEN (letter name plus 'maj7')	Cmaj7
MAJOR NINE (letter name plus 'maj9')	Cmaj9
NINE SUSPENDED (letter name plus '9sus')	C9sus
THIRTEEN (letter name plus '13')	C13

*NOTE: These are most of the *standard* chords used in church music (and in this folio) . . . but there are many others not included here!

The notation for 22 of the standard chord symbols appears below. Each chord may, of course, be *voiced* in more than one way. (In fact, all of the arrangements in this book include several *chord inversions*.)

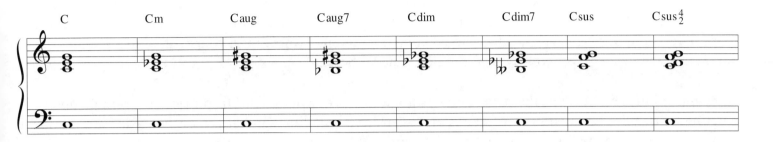

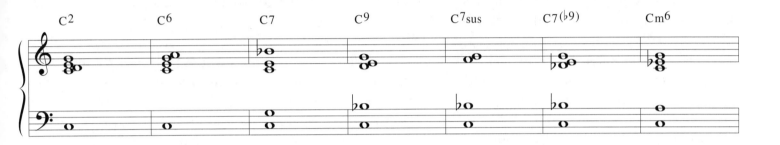

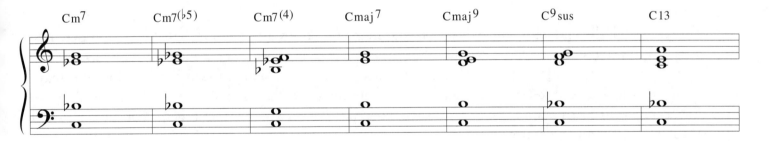

NOTE: Any chord symbol using TWO letter names *separated by a horizontal line* tells you that the lower letter is not the "root" of the chord.

For example:

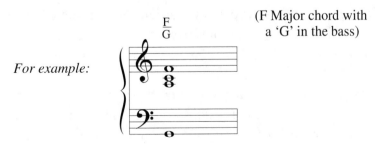

(F Major chord with a 'G' in the bass)

Blended Worship*

The term *BLENDED WORSHIP* refers to combining both traditional and contemporary elements in a single worship experience. Since music plays a big part in any service of worship, the *tasteful* blending of musical styles is critical in creating the environment for worship where hearts and minds are focused on God. And keyboard instruments are the *keys(!)* to creating a *natural flow* in worship… providing both beauty and balance. In Psalm 150, King David sets the precedent for praising God with instrumental music… trumpets, harps, lyres, tambourines, strings, flutes and clashing, resounding cymbals! (Of course, all of these sounds… and more… are made possible today by using electronic keyboards!)

Instrumental music often 'sets the stage' for worship. Many people have felt His presence so strongly upon entering Spirit-filled sanctuaries that feelings of despair have been lifted and attitudes changed. The emotional impact of instrumental music is nothing new, of course. When an evil spirit overtook Saul, David was summoned to play the harp to calm him (1 Sam. 16:23). And when Saul was feeling unworthy to become Israel's king, Samuel suggested that Saul return to his father's house, knowing that on the way he would encounter certain prophets playing instrumental music (tambourine, flute and harp). Sure enough, as Saul joined them in praise, his heart was changed (1 Sam. 10:5, 6).

Obviously, music is not an end in itself. When played *skillfully*, with *sensitivity* to the Holy Spirit, music becomes a *vehicle* for worship. However, the finest technical performance may not have any *heart*, and a willing (but unskilled) player may actually distract worshippers by a poor performance. King David (who taught Israel to worship) encouraged us to *play skillfully* (Ps. 33:3). In 2 Samuel 24:24, he also said that he would not offer the Lord anything that would cost him nothing. By now you must have figured out that I'm going to suggest the dreaded "P" word—*practice!* Please remember that when you are prepared (musically *and* spiritually), not only are you facilitating worship for the congregation, but it frees you to worship along with them.

Part of playing skillfully and with sensitivity is playing *tastefully*. For example, knowing when *not* to play is as important as knowing when to play! Don't use the same arpeggios in every song, don't play every *lick* you've ever learned (whether it fits the music or not), don't play each song in exactly the same style, and avoid playing several songs in the same key. (Yes, there really *are* more than two sharps and three flats in some church music!) Vary the instrumentation from song to song when possible. If you have an organ, acoustic piano and synthesizer, here are a few examples:

- ♣ When using piano and organ to accompany hymns, try having the organ drop out for one of the middle verses, or actually sing one verse a cappella.
- ♣ When using piano and synthesizer to accompany praise music, don't have them playing the same thing. Use the piano for the harmonic foundation of the song and have the synthesizer improvise a *fill* part on a solo instrumental setting (like flute, trumpet or strings). Try to match the *sound* with the song—by adding trumpet to *Majesty* or flute to *How Beautiful*, for example.
- ♣ On a more intimate song, use a simple keyboard accompaniment, or perhaps a nice acoustic guitar setting on the synthesizer to give it a more personal feel. (Be certain you are familiar with how a guitarist plays stylistically.)

In other words, use your imagination—*be creative!* Remember to make choices that make musical sense, using sounds that *enhance* the lyrics and style of the music. Creating new textures of sound helps to breathe new life into your music program. *"Sing to the Lord a new song"* is found several times in the Psalms and I believe that scripture applies to players as well as singers. (I also think that *new arrangements* may be considered *new songs*.)

---

* NOTE: Adapted from *THE CELEBRATION HYMNAL* WORSHIP RESOURCE EDITION (© 1997 by Word Music and Integrity Music)

As an arranger, putting well-known songs into new settings by creating different harmonies, new rhythmic patterns or changing meters is always challenging *(and a lot of fun!)*. The marketplace is filled with books to choose from, including arrangements for piano, organ or keyboard—solos, duets and ensembles. They are available at various levels of difficulty— from beginner to advanced, and some even have orchestra tracks. These books are created mostly for players who read music more easily than they play by ear or improvise, and may be used effectively as preludes, offertories, postludes or "special music." But since spontaneity and flexibility are often required, having church accompanists who can read music, have a good understanding of music theory, improvise *and* play by ear is ideal.

Most publishers include chord symbols in their songbooks, artist folios and choral music. They are very help-ful for an accompanist who may not be able to read the music note for note, and it gives them the option of adding guitar, bass and / or additional keyboard instruments. Keyboard players who can follow a chord chart are not limited to the printed page, and can be creative within the harmonic boundaries of the arrangement.

Even though praise bands and church orchestras have become more commonplace in many churches, key-board instruments remain the mainstay (or support) for all other instruments. In fact, several churches, par-ticularly in the mainline denominations, still exclusively use keyboard instruments. This means that one or more keyboards is almost always used when the service calls for music—preludes, opening hymns or songs, praise and worship choruses (including transitions and modulations), offertories, communion, invitations, special music, closing songs and postludes. As mentioned earlier, it is a good idea to vary the instrumentation and to involve several players when possible. After all, church should be a place to exercise our various gifts for the benefit of the Body. (And don't forget to include some of the younger piano students—*future church musicians!*) Not only is it good experience, but it helps them to feel that they're a part of what's happening in the church. There are many simplified arrangements of their favorite songs available. (As all piano teachers know, the sooner they can play something familiar, the better the chance that they won't become bored or discouraged and want to quit.)

Every generation writes its own songs, and, in blended worship, many churches incorporate several new songs (mostly choruses) per year into their worship. However, there is rarely adequate time on Sunday morning to teach them to the congregation. An effective (and subtle) way for the congregation to become familiar with a new melody is for a keyboard player to play it as a prelude, offertory, or other service piece. Then on another Sunday, the choir may sing it as a call to worship (if appropriate) or an anthem. The congregation will feel more comfortable with the song by the time it is their turn to participate. Generally, instrumental solos are arrangements of songs familiar to the congregation so that they can make a mental connection with the lyrics. If you have songwriters in your midst, playing original melodies as instrumental solos (or ensembles) should also be encouraged. Blended worship offers endless opportunities to those of us God has given musical gifts. Because the gifts are so *diverse*, but now *acceptable* in contemporary worship, our willingness to offer them to the Creator is surely pleasing to Him. (In fact, all of the arts—not just music—are being used more and more to enhance worship because they can *communicate*.)

Although the solo medleys in this book were created for acoustic piano, why not try adapting some of them to electronic keyboard as well… using settings with layered strings, for example. Because those of you using *Sunday Morning Blend* are at various stages of development in your individual music ministries, I have chosen not to talk specifically about the newest technology relating to electronic keyboards or to promote certain man-ufacturers. Once again, the possibilities are *infinite*—particularly with the availability of MIDI keyboards, addi-tional sound sources and authentic sampled sounds. The very latest and most innovative keyboards still need players who play *tastefully* and *skillfully*. If you are a pianist or organist who is intimidated by electronic key-boards, find someone who is knowledgeable and spend a little one-on-one time getting comfortable with the basics. Once you feel more secure, there will be no stopping you!